Acts of Contortion

Acts of Contortion

Anna George Meek

THE UNIVERSITY OF WISCONSIN PRESS

The University of Wisconsin Press
1930 Monroe Street
Madison, Wisconsin 53711

www.wisc.edu/wisconsinpress/

3 Henrietta Street
London WC2E 8LU, England

5   4   3   2   1

Printed in the United States of America

Library of Congress Cataloging-in-Publication Data
Meek, Anna, 1969–
    Acts of Contortion / Anna George Meek.
    pp. cm. — (Brittingham prize in poetry)
    ISBN 0-299-18260-6 (cloth : alk. paper)
    ISBN 0-299-18264-9 (pbk. : alk. paper)
I. Title. II. Brittingham prize in poetry (Series)
PS3613.E37 A28   2002
811'.6–dc21   2002005534

FOR MY PARENTS
Jay Meek and Martha George Meek

who have given me everything within their powers
of language and of love.

CONTENTS

ACKNOWLEDGMENTS

Grateful acknowledgment is made to the following publications, in
which many of the poems in this collection have previously appeared:

Crab Orchard Review: "Eating the Zoo"
Crazyhorse: "From the Force of Explosion," "Are You Now, or Have
    You Ever Been"
Cream City Review (25th Anniversary Issue): "Why the Uninhibited
    Suffer from Incontinence"
Hayden's Ferry Review: "An Old Man Performs Alchemy on His
    Doorstep at Christmastime"
Missouri Review: "Cookbook and Guide for Modern Living,"
    "Hand," "Langue de Femme"
Poetry: "Dexterity"
Water~Stone: "The Mural"

I did not write this book alone: thanks to Matthew Gladue, Julie Plaut,
Mary Durand, Phil Metres, Amy Breau, Maria LaMonaca, and Jay and
Martha Meek; these poems were shaped both by their critical readings
and by their friendships. Thanks also to the teachers who have encour-
aged me, especially Maura Stanton, Cathy Bowman, Susan Gubar,
Alice Fulton, Wayne Koestenbaum, and Langdon Hammer. Finally,
loving gratitude to the Bloomington and Twin Cities communities in
which this book was written, and to all of my family; they hold me
here in the place they have made where poems are possible.

I

THE HAND

Interior of the hand. Sole that has come to walk
only on feelings. . . .
.   .   .   .
That steps into other hands,
changes those that are like it
into a landscape:
wanders and arrives within them,
fills them with arrival.

—Rainer Maria Rilke, from "Palm"

Hand

Don't touch me. Don't
touch me here.

◡

Mahler's Ninth Symphony calls
for a thousand musicians: twenty-six bones
in each musician's hand. All that music!
All those moving parts.

◡

Carnal mathematics: babies soon discover
a strangeness before them, their digits
appearing like ugly slugs. This is knowledge.
Yes, Copernicus counted the stars
with his body. Anne Boleyn counted six
fingers; she was too much for the king
so he cut off her head. Minus one.

◡

Intimacy is the number ten.

◡

Some nights, I can't
control myself. I tend to get out of
the bed and shimmy into a skin
that dances the lambada
until the skin cries with love
for me. Morning, I shed
the awful thing, leave it weeping
on the floor.

What is the sound
that the violinist unfurls
opening from the wrist
like a question mark?

⌣

Speak to me in your vocabulary
of righteousness, of the sinister and the dexterous.
You, these extremes, are too clever for words.
Between left and right lives a sweet distance,
a yawn of no particular meaning.
Fill it with anything; fill it with me,
if you like.

⌣

In the story, push marries pull; they consummate
movement, but the child is stillborn. Pull
moves out. They may never meet again.

⌣

What if I professed my faithfulness,
offered you my hand? Would these lines
reach you? Nowadays, I need help
with laundry, dishes, sometimes waking,
a meager daily anatomy.
My body cannot answer for itself.
On the coastline, boulders scrape the water
like raw knuckles—not just a state
of injury, but a bold and brutal greeting.
I must believe that gifts are possible,
that tenderness is not unspeakable.
Read this as if I could hold you,
as if I could hold what I know.

A Political Poem

That evening, he was not allowed
into the battered women's shelter where he volunteered.
The screaming inside was intolerable.

Helpless, he painted the shelter's porch, stripping
old flakes from the cornices, the long boards,
politely quiet. His mind turned

to the possibility of his hands
around the neck of his violin, performing
angular scales—up, down, up—exactitude

that felt clean and fit. He imagined practicing
with the windows open, in mock privacy,
and the neighbors listening to the music

through their own open windows would feel
misleadingly welcome to it as if the young man
had left all his groceries out on the front lawn.

People like to help themselves, he believed,
to each other's company. But what
of his music could they know?

Outside on the porch,
he nicked the knuckle of his left thumb.
No national importance, surely,

but he knew that in the morning,
he would feel the sting. In his longing
to speak tenderly

through the violin,
his power to make an audience weep
ended here: he would never reconcile

the various articulations of injury—
Beethoven, and from inside, this
terrible shrieking.

Positions

He will not listen, and she leans
toward him over the restaurant table,
her hands over the silverware, spreading the napkin
wide, repositioning the ice water.

You don't know what it means
to me, but his face has turned toward
a woman for whom he feels
no sexual attraction but curiosity;

he watches her at the door, in a couple waiting
to be seated, and her hand spreads like an excitable bird
whose plumage fans over the center
of her lover's chest. I know that in such wilds,

in a dark bedroom, tinted by the green glow
of stereo dials, a man had told my friend
it won't bite, and the animal quivered
under her hand, the touch of its discovery,

but I heard about my colleague, an English teacher,
how her husband beat her at bedroom
games. Was it such an awful shock?
She taught Kate Chopin, her namesake,

as a matter of survival, I think, and the students read
her hollow blue face as the subject
of intensity, sleeplessness perhaps;
I am trying to imagine, pryingly,

the dirty moment he is holding her
thighs down in the down of the bed
and she is holding the mattress, face down,
and when he swings his hand above her,

I turn my head. I was never struck like that.
It seems silly, now, that last winter,
I wore black stilettos home
from a concert, their punctuation tipping me

precariously into ice and sudden
exclamation. The shoes can hold me
the way I'm too shy
to hold myself

in public; these broken histories
are what I read now in the tall leaning
of your body, akimbo and casting
its shadows away from me,

and against the etymology of your stance,
we are on speaking terms, terms even
of passion, sometimes hurtfulness,
and I do not know what place

or what ecstasy the pleasure and play
of a body can come home to, whether the sensual light
of an open window will keep the people
in a waiting room turned toward themselves,

or if the couple, ushered into the restaurant's back rooms,
will take their seats expectantly,
nodding with what they have not yet called love,
as if there were nothing to say.

From the Force of Explosion

Ava Gardner stood on the cliff's edge, waving
goodbye to Gregory Peck; the nuclear cloud
was ponderous, and lovely, as it drifted toward them
from a direction called America.

I saw the end of the world and it cost me
the price of a movie ticket. But there is really
no accounting for this end: I stepped into the light
and the streets became reanimated. Sprightly,

and mad, Fred Astaire told Ava
all that he had seen, the end of "mankind
as we know it," when what we know
is dramatic, full-scale,

a tidal swoosh of ballgowns carrying us away
into the next life. I was ten

when the oven blew up; and later, the state arsenal,
fifteen miles away: our dishes rattled with the noise
of those leaving their bodies behind. Beyond the theater,
distances fill with the force of explosion.

Far away from me,

my friend discovered flight from the twentieth floor;
impact at first was terrible and exciting and then,
I felt my life shaking outward, moving
through fifteen years to this moment, where the aftershocks

resound in a pianist, a twelve-year-old prodigy
whose plane today fell in flames over Long Island,
fell with two hundred other lives,

and I'm angry that at the turn
of this century, we are still vulnerable
to a force that is both distant and intimate,
that can overcome us in any state

of confidence or health. The sidewalks shine
with movie rain, whose black and white patter
will dry up in the afternoon light, just before
the evening show. I know the value

of this, the illusion that nouns can stand
for a collapse of cause or blame, but the names
mourn and *rubble* remain ludicrous, pathetically dainty.

No sound can fill the lengths between me
and the family of the young pianist better than the voice
of my own outbursts, crying

that I will always be a citizen of this distance
and the tremors I cannot exchange
for words or music: worthless, perhaps,
these losses that don't seem to mean anything.

Grief Becomes a Common Thing

However they sing their voices will glisten
in the soundmix. . . .
  —Adrienne Rich, "From Piercéd Darkness"

Someone is digging holes in your backyard
say my neighbors. Through the window,
the man is all writhing flannel, unfolding
when I approach, to become a man again:
our landlord. These are tomatoes,
he tells me, holding out nothing but his hands
above the dirt. His quick speech on varieties
shifts its weight, a story now about plants
and the old man down the street. He says: the old man
remembers when your house was his,
part of his garden. Planted fifty big potatoes.
Harvested fifty small ones.
That's not the way it happens now
(he says), because the old man's son may
have been wounded at Kent State, and now we live
on his father's land where nothing will grow.
Your house was built by a musician
(I'm hearing his voice diffuse through the grass),
but you wouldn't recognize it. It was smaller
and sinking into the mud, ship going down,
so she flew to Europe where her plane exploded
outside of Paris. Her headstone
came from the quarry—some good rock.
So did your house. The WPA had a field day
in this town. All those faces in the university
buildings come from the greatest artists
in Indiana. But I'm mixing things up
(his hand mixing air), of course; he sold the land

to the city just before the war. (I can't sleep
in the bedroom of a dead musician.)
He lost his wife last year—there was nothing
she didn't collect. (Yes.) Yes, I said,

I remember him on my stone porch,
showing me the auction pamphlet
and saying that the porcelain dolls
had been her favorite. Would I bid for one?
That was enough.

Secretly, I was sorry to be alone when the landlord left.
Now, I am standing above a hole
(I don't know what the landlord was digging for
in his hole in my backyard) where nothing
is growing behind the house of the dead musician
and I forget that he started by explaining
tomatoes that had never been there at all.
Wars were chiseled from this yard:
I won't sleep tonight. My heart is not my own.

Dexterity

Crab that crawls into my dream, clicking
across white porcelain tiles. Somewhere, fingers

are tatting, bone on bone, and the needles
articulate a fine point, lace: its syntax

made of exact little knots. Each key on a piano
can speak precisely of Bach,

as the clock skates the hours with ease, with skill. Blades
in a new razor carve out a chin

from the indeterminate beard. If the tips of tall firs
trace angular shapes above the night, their motion

will signal the sleepwalkers to step lightly
into their darkened gardens. There, fruit

is like the palm of a friend; and moths, like evening gowns
that flutter at the heels of the ballroom dancers.

Letter to the Man Who Watches Over Brains

What are you thinking
as you guard the Soviet portions
of brains once owned by Stalin, Lenin,
Rachmaninoff? Nestled under glass—
like domed paperweights where snow
tumbles down at the flick of a wrist—
these hemispheres once contained scenes
of beauty and torture. Brains
are historical sites: *this is where it all
happened*, where Athena
split open the cocoon, emerging
whole-spun, otherworldly.

                        Hello,
to the man who watches over brains,
hello, you who still carry
your own about town.
I know that burden too, driving
from the post office
to the grocery store for butter,
eggs, where the cashier
touches my hand gently, alighting
for an astonishing moment
to place the change in my palm,
so that I waltz to the car
with those I love
in mind.

        I imagine
it is difficult to sit with the brains
in such a featureless room, lit
by halogen lamps
without a single instrument
for embrace, not even
so much as a handshake.

I think I would tell them jokes,
read to them from the paper,
that they might come to be friends;
for them, I would go home whistling
the Second Symphony, respectful of spaghetti
and sponges, and for them, would never again eat
gelatinous desserts, although
they have been removed
from all that we know.

Poise

They cannot cry out to each other
over the girders and cranes. A foreman conducts
the walls into the air; they lift and drift away
like receding voices. Across the street, I am no more
than a cat in a high window, watching
one man, my favorite, playfully giving his partner
the finger. When he finally puts it away, I feel exposed.
He knows something, knows my sudden self-consciousness,
vertigo, he looks straight into my building, seeing me,
our meeting twelve stories over city traffic
still and suspended. Balance. We can't drop our eyes.
We're listening for the sound of weight, and distance.

House

Last night, I dreamed that I lived
in an attic room, and then, for no reason,
I moved across the street to another
attic room. The woman who took my old attic
seemed pleased. From my window, I watched her sleep
when her house caught fire. Everyone escaped
except her. She burned to death with the house.

Previously knowing only the projects,
the Richardses' daughter crayoned the word *hosue*,
an inadvertent inversion, the awkward exchange, moving
here into there. This is, perhaps, how mishaps
occur: hammering dark nails into dark shingles,
the family and the volunteers built the new rooftop all afternoon—
it's not the equal and opposite physics you think, no
hammer plus thumb, exact injury, nor things
that fall down, which Newton confused with epiphany.
Below us in their kitchen, Mr. and Mrs. Richards
laughed and opened their imaginary cabinets. *Stánza*

is the Italian for *room*, a hollow that stands patient
for our restlessness to fill it. Equal to:
a patient balance dish, its desire
for literal translation, to make words worth the weight
of understanding. Mrs. Richards and I swap
stories. She works at the 7-Eleven (its own
imbalance), tells me that in New York, an old woman
won lottery millions and gave it all away
to her local church. That's not my life,
she says to me, but I guess it could have been.

Why can't I say it outright? We shifted
uncomfortably on the roof, the whole crew straddling
above the living room now as on a boat
or an ark above invisible water
precisely at the moment that miles away,
flood cracks opened in the dikes in North Dakota
and my own family was losing its home to the river.
Fire has no analogue. Water swells beyond
any definition given to it. People live in poverty
in the falsehood of fair economy.
A word shifts over the alphabet's shaky tectonics,
and precisely at that moment,
we can't exchange our lives for any other, displaced
by nightmare, coincidence, inexplicable accident.

II

ITS INJURY

injury [L., *in-*, not, lacking, without + *jurare*, to pronounce a ritual formula]

pronounce [L., *pronunciare,* to speak or shout in public]

—*The American Heritage Dictionary*

Protest Movements

In a way, I've been sworn to secrecy
about when she arrived at the shelter,
how long she'd been clean, a while,
how much she loved her little daughter
who liked me, or my shoes.
Or about the poems she showed me
while we sat at the kitchen table,
about her stories, which made me
go home and hold myself for a long time.
Once, she saw me across the street
and before either of us could think,
she'd called out to me, by name, and I'd
waved back. Immediately,
we were both concerned for her safety.
She was with a man. Maybe
I became a waitress, or a bank teller,
or a sister's neighbor. One night,
not long after—I can't tell you this—
she didn't come back. I knew only
when I read about her in the newspaper, a story
by someone else. I don't care about the rules.
I've got to write this because I want the chance
to grab her by the hand and say to her
don't go. Please
take care of yourself.

Epigraphs

*The decentered subject dwells . . . in the rhetorical space of the self/other encounter
in which the dynamics of deliberation on matters personal and social proceeds.*
  —Calvin O. Schrag, *Communicative Praxis and the Space of Subjectivity*

During a Minnesota cold snap, you have to run backwards in order to spit.
  —*The Insider's Guide to Minneapolis/Saint Paul*

Protest at the Saint Paul capitol: expression, excretion,
we chant, we yell. Bodies come forward. Bodies
retreat. The composition of urine is part mineral,
part acid, it eats through the sidewalks
we own together. Our composition is water,
and anger, shouting: people sleep in churches,
lotteries for mats on the floor, and damn,
it's cold, communal cold, cold to make iron burn
on the backs of the naked. Here, we are fatigue
and parka; this coat from Indonesia, that one
made in Bangladesh, country of rain, of *vartan bhanji*,
no longer Pakistan which is no longer
India. *Independent* says the Encyclopædia
Britannica. And we believe: everyone is entitled
to decent housing. When the cops arrive, we borrow
our chants from older fights: *hell no! We*
the expressive subject is indeed strong, now a multitude
—and salivating. From somewhere, the sub-
lingual gland arcs a globbet of enzymes, bacterial
colonies, and it arrives at the government steps
out of nowhere, odd, for a moment like seemingly
irrelevant information. Ice hangs from our mouths,
words of strangers sting our purpling lips.
This winter is long. We call and respond.

Why the Uninhibited Suffer from Incontinence

They drink milk from the carton
in the checkout lane, loosen
their clothing in public
and jiggle. Wantonly, they pour spirits
onto the reeking front lawn
where the dog sleeps epicureanly
all night. I prefer the ocean
for pulling itself in. All bodies
of water know tension
makes shape happen; retention
holds our dreaming, its watery terrors
cuppable even as we walk among the daylight,
bloated with bad nights
and full consciences.
The resistance of the water
against the canoe I rowed last night,
in my sleep, pushes on my day.
I send myself out, and withdraw.
No wonder my students confuse
loose and *lose,* that one droplet rolling
away, into the difference between feeling free
and not knowing oneself at all. One unrequited summer,
I fled to Paris, no—I *flew* to Paris,
and woke at hot midnight
to the sound of drunken men outside
laughing and yelling to one another,
losing their pants
and urinating into the open street.

Offices of the Only-Children

In the city, the only-children are grown
and haunted by their aging parents,
a sadness they know as loyalty.
They are taking their posts at desks
like bored nightwatchmen
vigilant for what doesn't happen
and dreading it. On the evening train,
at stops where no one gets off,
the doors hang open too long,
like the mouth of a man who realizes
he's got nothing to say, after all,
then closes it, moving on in his thoughts
to the end of the day, each commute
back to his own children
a quiet betrayal.

Ghostly Women

Each wedding, haunted. The phantom of a poulterer
    runs into the bridal shop
gathering his chickens among the pale skirts.
    He's named his favorite hen *Giselle,*
and he's calling and calling her, but she is gone.

In the mirror, the girls twist and look over their shoulders.
    No one there. This white is the shy suggestion
of a loss all brides allegedly desire. I am wearing my great-
    grandmother's dress this spring,
my mother's and my mother's mother's. Genealogy always makes me

stutter. On the girls' bosoms, sequins repeat themselves:
    your family has spoken you,
again and again, every woman an open vowel at the end
    of her dress. The girls cluck and fluster
in their shiny things. We can't know what will come from them.

I cherish the old cenotaphs. Appetent, my lover and I
    strip howling, trying to name
the absences, and in our longing, honor them.

Unsigned Watercolors Over the Bar

Alone, she is pushing herself away from the bar,
refusing the brass nuzzling against her chest.
Her blouse leans forward, mourns the touch,

and falls back again. Flawed, lit up,
these paintings mock her. They are of nothing.
Guttural strokes; blue with its mouth full;

red that sings deafly over the rib-shattering bass
pumping through all the drinkers. We believe
vibration is something we all have in common.

Laughing, a man throws his hands in the air
like he's been saved. In booth six,
you're telling me again how your father took you for burgers

in order to mention your mother's chances
for survival. I'm distracted: effusions of smoke
through barlight, shapes of memory that heave,

and heave. I know you by these repetitions,
your signature. They are words for what I want
to identify: symptoms. The lonely woman dissolves

into noise by the door. You can see her
escape the color-by-numbers, percentage of pink,
yellow, rain, all predictions, screw meteorology,

which is maybe why she came to the bar,
for chance. Not exactly knowledge, not what we hope
to learn. You notice I've carried the same book

with me for a week, leaning into it whenever,
to visit its common gestures. *Take it*. But we're slipping
outside of ourselves, beer after beer. The bottle bones.

Around your swelling fear the room twists, badly made.
The watery night skids away on pale verbs.
Not even this noun will steady you, love.

The Pacifist Dreams of an Apocalypse

Fresh Broccoli Soup Can Be Ready In An Hour
  —a front page newspaper headline

No one will get hurt in the green world.
The wealthy summer will spend its humidity
generously, fresh silver in the morning streets.
But you must prepare for it. A woman arrives
at the shelter wearing fingerprint-black
from the angry night. She has her purse
and her son. In the shelter's kitchen
the foods imitate a healed body: a head of lettuce,
and, of course, the bronchial vegetables,
cauliflower, broccoli. That life is spacious
and deep-breathing, believing that the coming revolution
will not be violent, will appear like splendid harvest
and all things rusting will move again with a little
olive oil. Steel yourself for the day
the broken man, who sobs and threatens you
through the telephone, receives a cup of green tea
and is soothed. Prepare, in our new millennium, for the end
of desires for which we hate ourselves.
Expect bounty. At this very hour, whole armies
are serving asparagus, repairing their nations
of grief, of the terrorism of illness, of beatings.
Sit down, says the shelter worker.
Let me fix you something.

The Performance of What We Don't Have

The old Greek mask was a kind of megaphone.
  —Thomas McGrath, interview

Everywhere, in telephones, is the night
where the body cannot rise up and reach
for what little might be held closely.
The dead stiffen in deliberate silence,
but the living must give up their voices
and send them out as a measure
of distance. After the evening rush hour,
on a downtown bus, a woman in heavy make-up
is yelling her monologue, clearly tired
of her own make-believe, no longer able
to pretend she is on her way home from work,
toward dinner, toward any consummation
of the middle-class. She is tired of the phony economics
in exchanged glances.

Telephones are another false promise.
From the next room, the assistant hears
Watson, come here; I need you,
a triumph this century responds to
when, stupid to sidewalk traffic,
a public telephone begins to ring. Though startled,
one man on a nearby heating grate doesn't turn
to look. It's not for him. But he jumps,
a passing businessman jumps, an old woman
pushing an empty stroller, all
jump, each of them like concert pianists
trying to gouge out from the piano keys
handfuls of Chopin, an act so horrifying
it makes them leap to do it.

This isn't a story about how the dead
call up their ex-lovers, too nervous
to visit in person. The dead know better.
Wanting for nothing, they keep silent.
I've spent some time eating soup and bread
with those among the living who must lie
about their pasts; they have nothing
but stories, and I know only what their lives
haven't been. Before dawn, members of congress
are phoning their clandestine affairs,
dramas of heartache and concealed identity;
in theory, if they were closer, they wouldn't be
talking at all, but that's the common trick
of neglect, like a teenager at the corner
sucking at a cigarette behind her palm.
If I were that girl on the corner, I'd say:

I am speaking outside myself
so that you might hear what I need.

In Response to a Woman Who Asked Me
What Stories I Would Tell My Daughter,
if I Had One

Oh!
  —Dorothy, arriving in Oz

When she learns her house has come down,
the old woman at the shelter is confused, she can't read
the city letter, she's begging me, *Why an old lady's house?*

The other women are hiding
behind the door, listening. They're gossipy here; inappropriately,
in a few minutes the radio soprano will kill herself

for love. Pity she's condemned herself to that,
when a heroine could go somewhere, the Riviera, the Pyramids,
land of ruby and gingham, become changed, even the pigs

would seem like friends. I know it's common
in these situations for the man to strangle the dog

first. This time, forty of them, their bodies
rotting right through the floorboards. She says she's decided:
No more dogs. She's not

kidding. Behind the door, one woman laughs, seized
by the hard fantasy of her dt's and their loony
nervous characters: Cold Sweat, Night Sweat, and
Shaky. No, no—*migraine* the women teach me
to say, because this word makes her

feel better. They emerge to say
they're sorry. Once upon a time,
I knew a young man

who was too forceful, but nothing
like what the women here have to tell

about themselves, nothing
like what we heard through the windowpanes
that night when she wandered out: you can be

almost anyone trying to go home
under a weight, as the old woman was, when the evening breeze

found her body
brittle. Hollowed her out

with its open, frightened vowel.

III

AND THEIR DIFFICULT MUSIC

The only state that is as anomalous as pain is the imagination . . . the imagination is bound up with compassion . . . the imagination has an inherent tendency toward largesse and excess . . . the work of the imagination is not here and there, now on, now off, but massive, continuous, and ongoing, like a watchman patrolling the dikes of culture by day and by night.

—Elaine Scarry, *The Body in Pain*

Orchestration

In the orchard, red apples
weigh their riches, overfull—
that is, if we can call them
red: or crimson? Bordeaux?
We can't know. We must desire precision

and love approximation. The apples
negotiate heaviness with other apples;
suspended, they ponder the leaves
of music that brush and bend,

in the orchard. More precisely, we call it:
counterpoint, musical lines twining around
an imagined center like vines. Ripe
notes, tones of wine. Or blush?
At the center of the orchestra
that plays just for him, a dictator

has peaches for breakfast: rosé, almost the color
of the pig his servant arranges
to have slaughtered today. But the hungry

are negotiating to rise up against the dictator,
they overthrow him and feed themselves
from his orchards, where the bees sing
fourth species counterpoint. Where
is the edge of color? The edge
of a spreading bruise, a neighborhood,
a body in sex? We must desire
precision and love

proximity. A plane taxies out, the bus
pulls in. Passengers lug their stiff torsos like cellos
from their seats—fine instruments,
all. One woman
already at the curb, negotiating
her luggage. Then,

her gesture: it probably means
she's hailing a taxi, her arm reaching up
to pluck fruit from a tree.

An Old Man Performs Alchemy
on His Doorstep at Christmastime

Cream of Tartar, commonly used to lift meringue and
angel food cake, is actually made from crystallized fine wine.

After they stopped singing for him,
the carolers became transparent in the dark,
and he stepped into their emptiness to say
he lost his wife last week, please
sing again. Their voices filled with gold.
Last week, his fedora nodded hello to me
on the sidewalk, and the fragile breath
of kindness that passed between us
made something sweet of a morning
that had frightened me for no earthly reason.
Surely, you know this by another name:
the mysteries we intake, exhale, could be
sitting on our shelves, left on the bus seat
beside us. Don't wash your hands.
You fingered them at the supermarket,
gave them to the cashier; intoxicated tonight,
she'll sing in the streets. Think of the old man.
Who knew he kept the secret of levitation,
transference, and lightness filling a winter night?
—an effortless, crystalline powder
that could almost seem transfigured from loss.

Molecular Lives

Struck by lightning, the tightrope aerialist
      was suddenly overwhelmed by his life;
small beads of quartz formed under his nails.
      It's not that unusual for a body
to conduct high currents and become something

      else. Strangers to each other,
three women attended a science lecture on the aerialist,
      but flung themselves
from the auditorium where they met and formed
      a rock band in the atrium.
One woman knew all about electricity and Chopin.
      She had just finished crying
over an onion, small kitchen sadness before dinner,
      when the radio pianist faltered,
and stopped. Ravenous for the music,
      her cat had fed
from the power cord on a delicious, unbearable
      stillness. So she plugged in.
Here, she said, I will take from molecular life
      its screeching, its desperate bonds,
its chemically imbalanced subway crazies yelling *shit*
      for seven stops before deciding
that the eighth counts as an arrival. All right,

I'll swear to the truth of it: I'm making up these stories
      on a night of high honor
after a man appeared at my bedroom window in the dark
      with a knife, with a bouquet, no,
with a cigarette whose glow I remember like I remember
      my love for my parents, for music,
for this life: searing truths whose material body

sometimes seems a fiction.
I have no evidence. But I screamed until my skin
    galvanized. Safety, tonight,
is clear as a gem, a rare specimen of catastrophe.

The Mural

The land teems with village and marketfare,
rugs, brooms, hare-lipped fish, roast pigs
stuffed like purses, the deaf man
driving his goats through the booths
where a stray pauses to eat the beads
of a gypsy whose nose ring flares up in anger
like a bull's. *Tell the King,*
it's from a friend, the shadow whispers
and is gone, leaving the young mutton-legged page
bewildered and trembling. Far away, the travelers
drawn in the lower-right-hand corner know nothing
of these secrets, as, from their cliff, they watch
the drunken sea teeter and fall
at the shores of the village isle. And yet

from here in the museum, the world in the mural
is actually uninhabited: streets appear abandoned,
houses huddled for safety away from the deserted cliffs,
and I can hear the mural echo in these halls,
empty with closing time. But despite appearances,
it does feel that the days outside are built right to the edge,

thronging with mysterious, invisible ongoings:
people delivering messages in the dark
to others unsure of how to take them, while lonely hands
converse in silhouette under the flickering projection light.
As with fantasy, always the uncertainty
of romance in the movie theaters, always the groping
for underthings. And the works of art
we alone rise to, the portraits we scrub mornings,
pamper and position like beautiful,
unbruised fruit, will speak to us

from the bathroom mirror and say
what? How much can we see from here?
The mind gallops into anything,

tumbling the still lives where the fruit
is gobbled by the goats, and the chickens
fluster like sheets from a bed,
and all tightly-clasped timidity is undone.
If only the charge on that kingdom
were so easy from this world,
although arrival anywhere is accidental,
pure chance, any midwife could tell you that.
Only one whoops! and the fantastic occurs; it breeds
everywhere, the walls and tables. Some nights

on the telephone, I hear the long-distance
whinnying of an uninvited voice
speaking to whomever is out there,
like a sightless fortune teller or oracle, saying
we must always be suspicious of the empty village,
no matter how we arrived, strapped
to the mast, shipwrecked wailing and blind,
each of us, explorers.

The Hurdy-Gurdy Player

My apartment, my lot, and this guy
is standing in front of my car,
says he's a lawyer and he's instructing me
how to back out, and I say
get out of my way, I know
how to drive—but I really don't
tell him that, and I pull away
hating being a small, young woman,
almost as much as I hate lawyers,
and the car shifts peevishly into second.
It whines an unusual descant
to my muttering; there are a lot
of alternate names for this lawyer
and his pushy fat
asterisk, most of which my poem
won't say with grace.

The restaurant is a good place
for her portrait to hang, the porky
pretty hurdy-gurdy player
who fills her pink dress
with what might seem at first
like a gawky, lumbering joy,
but that's a firm grasp she's got
on the hurdy-gurdy, almost fisted.

Finally, on the way home,
I'm no longer angry.
Driving a standard is an exact music,
like Bach or Schoenberg, both scientific
and passionate, my assertive shift
into fourth, swift, inscriptive,
which the car registers with speed,
inarticulate, and such
a strange instrument to play.

Cookbook and Guide for Modern Living

Any woman can be an artist and enjoy the artist's thrill without stirring out of her kitchen. . . . One who appreciates and distinguishes between the different flavors in cookery . . . has culture, which is a sensibility to the finer and more beautiful things in this world.
   —Mabel Claire, *Macy's Cookbook and Kitchen Guide for the Busy Woman,* 1932

INTRODUCTION: GLOSSARY OF TERMS, MEASURES

Let it be daily living, a preparation for graciousness.
Simmer is light heat that barely moves
the long, slow evening into summer night.
Stir and *stew* are the gentle cousins
of *beat* and *boil* whose movements are violent,
measures that sometimes need to be taken,
and *dredge, mask,* and *marinate* speak
quietly of cover, hiddenness, drowning.
Good cooking is civil, cultured.

A RECIPE

Three parts gentle goose, one part young
greens, one part milk will make any woman
a fine meal, delicate, and well-rounded.

COOKING CORNISH GAME HEN

I spread its legs apart, grabbing each
knobby stub, dancing awkwardly
with a woman smaller, younger than I,
and too politely lead her across the room, lit
by heat and beading water.
The kitchen is a kind of dance floor—
the touch of clammy skin,
gentle, misleading, but the movements
calculated, in whose heat

one overcomes shyness. Limber,
I stoop to the oven light and swivel
to the oil, grazing the pots, the mustard,
that scuttle from my hands. I check the bird;
I am too strong, reaching inside,
waiting for the odors to rise.

MANAGING THE SERVANTS

The cat brushes against my leg, crying
to be fed. He has heard the opener,
a grinding I recognize as the sound
my husband makes asleep, clenching his teeth
in night-horror. He must obey
his own fevers, leaping into wakefulness
as if it would save him. I watch him
break the surface, shake the dream
from his hair and hands, and he holds
my arm until he drifts away again. The cat
is more persistent; he tries to run out
when the boys come to mow the lawn.
The landlord has hired them, but
I am uncomfortable when they are here;
at night in my dream, I let the cat out
and the boys come in, and letting go
of our machines and nightmares,
we would drink coffee, watch the dark water
slip from the carafe.

Are You Now, or Have You Ever Been

Respond with a lie: I've never been a violinist.
Or a woman. I'm a confidently gay
blueberry farmer who watches foreign films
in his underwear, secretly preferring
strawberries. I won't admit this
to my lover, loyalist of the bright and purely blue.
Our years together have been breathless,
unquestionable; but our public lives
are something else. When he answers
the phone, I watch as he is pulled into another
voice, not one of deceit, but rather
a post to which he's been appointed, abruptly,
one he accepts with honor, and formality.
Hanging up, he relaxes into one of his former lives,
only briefly fearful of what passes, at this moment,
for himself. Soon he reaches for the body
of his violin, which he will interrogate
for confessions of music—even in the lie
a truth surfaces; yes, I'm still an American
blueberry farmer, but oh how I love the Russians:
Tchaikovsky, Stravinsky, Shostakovich.

Our neighbors have named their many cats
cat, in every language of their ancestries.
Voices across the coming storm cry *Gato! Katze!*
The cats answer to none of them.
At dusk, my lover and I are not what we've been
to each other in the hours of containment,
its daylit expressions. While the rain stutters
over the roof and into the blue eyes nestled in our fields,
the forecaster lovingly touches the silhouettes
of meteorology, of our country. He's ready
to tell you everything he knows:

all weather is immigrant, the whorls
now spinning into your neighborhood
will make love to your trees
and move on. In the morning,
this land will be changed,
willfully congregating upon itself
the leafy tongues of gold
and red.

Eating the Zoo

Because of the danger involved in killing them, the lions and tigers survived, as did the monkeys, protected apparently by the Darwinian instinct of the Parisians.
　—Alistair Horne, on the Paris siege of 1871, *The Terrible Year*

In *la ville lumiere,* the terrible weight of light
and truth consumed itself in fat bustiers and balls;
the prosperity of champagne

corseted poverty, revolution. I am reading about the Paris siege
as this March afternoon throws grids across
the unmapped carpet of the library,

every moment of our sudden warm weather
graciously unquestioned by any of the open window's
outdoor voices. Still, the papers say that lions

are coming down from the California hills,
and the 'City that Reads' has swallowed another library.
It was a terrible year.

In 1871, the Hotel de Ville burned,
and mobs tore the imperial eagles down from the palace,
tossing their busts of the emperor into the Seine.

The communards said: the worker
can hurl his own art into the river.
Have we not been a country

borrowing against ourselves, our drunkenness,
and secret syphilitic decay? Delirious,
purulent, Baudelaire crawled to the bookshelf

for his books of poetry so he could remember
his own name—they must have recognized themselves,
the *citoyens,* when they began to eat the zoo

and its wilderness: parrot, camel, antelope,
feeding on exotica and unrestraint,
anything that would not eat them first—

and in the Champs Elysée, the starving public
squawked and pranced through the city.
Four shots each to fell the famed twin elephants,

Castor and Pollux, for whom they'd hungered
all along, their great trunks a delicacy
only legend knew. Forty francs a pound.

The *citoyens* peered into the monkeyhouses
to read their own names. The monkeys
peeled open their bananas like garden flowers,

considered them, considered the yellow eyes
of the Frenchmen beyond the bars.
Who would kill a poem? they chattered.

That is, if they could catch it.

Langue de Femme

langue de femme [Fr., language, tongue + woman]
a grass with a long, sharp blade, commonly called *quiver-grass*

In the shelter's kitchen, we gather in a salty afternoon

light, shaky comfort. Almost always someone
on the hallway phone crying.

The boiling water tattles and sighs. We argue
about legalizing pot, we argue pain medication, not pain
medication; I'm the only one here never knifed. Sheila

tells half a story—none of us really understands
how to use the new oven, distracted. Apologizing

Joan steps out for a "cigarette," knows one can't always
use real names
for things. Just after she leaves, a few tremors

of gossip about her at our unsteady table, edgy,
when the unwatched flower vase startles over the rim,
$\qquad\qquad$ and the room falls

quiet. Then,
lily tongues everywhere, broken glass, greenery, the table shaking
under the nervous weight of our laughter. Langue

de femme: we are rich beyond shattering.
The whole mess vibrating, one long neck, exposed
and reedy in this sweet tension. The moment bends easily now

to picking up shards under our table of stories. It's a two–story
shelter. Carrie starts talking

sharp fractals: rape upon rape, strangulation, strange angles
into ordinary life, her husband coming home, then coming home
again, with the knife. The first, or second time? I ask. *No,*

that was before: Carrie choking, brittle. Sheila
yells for help; she's growing
red tendrils from her hand over the glass. I push
to the cabinet for bandages, but it jams shut,

we pry it open with wild knives, and it gives
gladly. Beautiful isn't the word.
We waver over it; vague, unparsed.

Vision of Agape

I felt myself invaded by a power which, though I consented to it,
was irresistible and certainly not mine. For the first time in my life,
I knew exactly—because, thanks to the power, I was doing it—
what it meant to love one's neighbor as oneself.
   —W. H. Auden, describing his vision of *agape*

In the back of the truck of Afghani refugees,
a woman's body opens

for birth—an edge, and the folds of her
public widening. The Americans arrive
at the border, they hold the woman's thighs
in this world, as another chestnut male enters

it: the child crowning: as royal as
a plush early light—this metaphor will carry him
across. From under the veil, the woman screams

let us cross! let us cross! And in another
language: she wants
out. The Americans are pushing
to the dangerous center, in camouflage,
we cannot tell their bodies

from land: the consent to dissolve, to be
absorbed, the consent of the ongoing story to absorb
another unbearable evening—cool,

disengaged. Inside America, inside an American,
waiting at a bus stop, a cell divides imprecisely;
it's more than this guy can stand, not to tear away
the coverings from the old Muslim beside him,
he must not be betrayed. The edges

change. The story is porous,
skin doesn't end here, instead, the old man's forehead
tears open, and bleeds. Citizens

disperse. We already know
how difficult this is to admit, the letting in, the risk
of infection. The story cuts
to later that afternoon when the old man
dies. It lays us wide open. From inside

these lines—if we can trust
what such a sweet voice has to say
about the regions of power and their neighbors, those
who have not

consented; loss; and
the Dead—the voice cries: we were crowned
in another country. Could we disguise
that we remain—or I, or I, impossible
monolith—could I remain

an alien to my own
imprecise conscience? I beg you,
Émigré, crawl across my borders.
Sneak your old mother into my heart.

IV

ACTS OF CONTORTION

(I am large—I contain multitudes.)

—Walt Whitman, *Leaves of Grass*

Acts of Contortion

Precision comes to town as a circus contortionist;
her body is lace, an intricate x, she's an artist
of script, she wants to bring
pleasure to audiences of children everywhere.
Loving them, she twists, baroque and bearing
down into her chest like a cellist
grinding with the care
of things well said. The articulate carnival is molded
from vague feeling. She knows
the desires, this night, her spectators will keep.
The children are frightened. She's folded
a letter to them that they'll read
years from now as adults, when they'll weep
in their lovers' arms with relief.

⌣

We are not fragmented but multiple:
a man receives his brother's lung
still filled with night air and honeysuckle;
at last, the man revives and exhales:
the hospital room billows with fragrances
of his brother's former solitude.
Such a thin membrane between words,
between words and our eardrums,
fluttering like backporch moths.
Almost transparent, the hanging curtains
that divide hospital emergencies,
shadows appearing to the broken hand,
the tonsillitis. Tonight, shadows
are what these share.

In my fiercest solitude, I drive
into town to sit down among people
I don't know. To hear rooms full
of talk and other lives: the cost
of coffee; a brother's stocks;
autumnal lovemaking. I know
the body's a seasonal shelter.
In spring, soft, fleshy earth; in winter, bone.
Alone, I knock through my nouns
like quarry rubble. Say: *shelter;*
say we are vulnerable, admit
the house will wash away.
I'm sleepless tonight. If I say that we all live
together, perhaps we'll keep until morning.

       ⌣

A woman is struck by the end
of a blunt instrument. Its literalness.
I know her, and her name,
the word that grabs her
attention, grazes her turning face
like laundry arching in the wind.
And she laughs. She knows my name.
All afternoon, we sit at the shelter's table
and hand words to each other.
Soft gifts from our mouths, a grace
we call exchange. We touch
what I need, what she may need too.
Yet her swollen wrists speak this much:
Our names will not save us.

Two men collide on a busy sidewalk.
Their argument is a city of words,
a difficult community. Iffy transportation.
Sure, the verbs'll get you around
if they come on time, if they run at all.
Commuters. Poverty. The nouns are rude
to each other. They live among exclamation.
One man's tongue is a flasher, suddenly nude,
then darting away, and back again. Appalled,
aroused, the other man pursues, he's dropping
his articles, losing whole sentences, picking up others.
The men are rattling in their dentin tenements.
Watching them shake, passersby
might mistake them for lovers.

ᴗ

Fall is manifold. Letters from the trees
litter the hours. The empty places
are now populous with gold.
And moving: things are migrating in me.
I'm dusk inside, changing light, fresh cold;
outside, I read my neighbors' faces
not for meaning—not mine to take—
but for understandings that border
theirs: the quarter moon that we agree
to know. The order
of days. The possibilities of snow.
Passing me, a stranger appears to force shyness,
fear through the narrow neck of *hello.*
And her word multiplies into color.

The day my friend leaped from himself
was beautiful. It was elsewhere:
in my spring, water pulled itself down
from the branches like silver. In his own February,
so generous, he became selfless. Fifteen years
now, this slow thaw of missing him.
Far away, both then and now, I have had to make
my seeing: in the window, he is framed
and filled with light. The day is awful.
He's thinking of his family. Perhaps of me.
Although it's ourselves we remember,
we are each other's multiple.
I'm angry with him, with the winter I carry.
I'm tired of catching my friends falling as I sleep.

⌣

These nine months, a childhood friend has three
hearts, and smaller limbs she grows within; she
accepts the strangers under her elastic skin.
Her generous body aspires to open. I remember
how she negotiates the piano, her twin
hands arguing over the keys, and later
how she eats a silent dinner with them both,
each hand all cried out. On the phone,
she speaks to me like this: *we sometimes feel—*
we have always known—. I listen, cleave to similar notions.
She believes in simultaneity. Alone
and landlocked, I think of an infantile joke,
when just miles from the untold ocean,
she laughs, she laughs, she laughs.

The orchestra adores his good hand
which conducts us now beyond palsy
into our loving, ecstatic responses:
friction, vibration, percussion.
Instruments lavish the empty hall with a grand
force, back sprain, the songs of rapture
and carpal tunnel; a sweet creek
of silver slivers runs in my fingertips.
The bad hand doesn't speak
to the piano any longer, a stranger
by his side, but we love that hand too,
it listens quietly. The hall is safe.
Excessive, we overextend him our hands.
We hundred chafe as intimates.

⌣

Some pains in the Palladium:
blue veins through white marble, marks
of both loss and making. The right arm arcs
across her torso, and the figure's hand
gives shelter to her naked stone.
I love this story: an entire land
saved by a statue, and when I was younger,
I thought, *it sounds true*.
I've often imagined her voice to be beautiful.
It says: each of you a citizen,
you who live here with me.
It says: do not be afraid to speak as *We*
and know that the city will always be within
and around you.

Behind the scalpel, the flesh unzips.
Its tender interior engorges with desire
for the air, our bodily eros:
we could come out of ourselves.
We could consummate all distance
in its unbearable forms: unlikeness,
incongruity, momentary error whose lips
barely part to take us in.
We could know strangeness.
And in the sleep of this injury, the body
presses outward past the fingers
of the surgeon, an instance
of touch, music more than what the skin
allows, even our own dark sinews.

⌣

Bless the hand and its painstaking
acts of contortion, dozens of them
torqued and clawing at the necks
of violins in an exquisite forcefulness
their owners call Rimsky-Korsakov
or some other music that's difficult
to finger-spell. Bless the signature,
the love sonnet, the hand clutching the heart.
Bless every embrace. Bless the strain
of lovemaking, and the injuries it sustains.
Bless the breadloaf baked
and gladly eaten with strangers, with those
who have no home but here:
in distance, in touch, in everything generously spoken.

THE BRITTINGHAM PRIZE IN POETRY

The University of Wisconsin Press Poetry Series • Ronald Wallace, General Editor

Brief Landing on the Earth's Surface • *Juanita Brunk*
Philip Levine, Judge, 1996

And Her Soul Out Of Nothing • *Olena Kalytiak Davis*
Rita Dove, Judge, 1997

Bardo • *Suzanne Paola*
Donald Hall, Judge, 1998

A Field Guide to the Heavens • *Frank X. Gaspar*
Robert Bly, Judge, 1999

A Path Between Houses • *Greg Rappleye*
Alicia Ostriker, Judge, 2000

Horizon Note • *Robin Behn*
Mark Doty, Judge, 2001

Acts of Contortion • *Anna George Meek*
Edward Hirsch, Judge, 2002